8 mistakes even the most experienced online entrepreneurs make

... and how to make money avoiding them

By Ricco Mortensen

Published by the Ricco Mortensen Foundation.
First edition.

upon any purchase from the companies. While the author and publisher take no responsibility for the business practices of these companies and or the performance of any product or service, the author or publisher has used the product or service and makes a recommendation in good faith based on that experience.

For more information, please visit
www.riccomortensen.com.

ISBN 978-87-998835-2-3.

Table of Contents

Why you need this book

I'm so excited that you've decided to learn more about how to run an online business that actually makes you money.

With this book I'm going to give you a good entrepreneurial kick in the behind — aha moments included. Whether you're just starting up or have had your business for years, the insights in this book will positively impact your business.

In this book you'll get the answers to all 8 mistakes that I see even the most experienced entrepreneurs making far too often.

These are mistakes I see time and time again as I teach and mentor ambitious entrepreneurs.

In fact, it's due to these mistakes that so many entrepreneurs fail to succeed with their businesses. In the pages that follow, I intend to change this.

By the time you've finished this book, you'll know how to get started making the necessary changes in your business so that you can finally earn good money and live the entrepreneurial life you dream of.

Enjoy reading.
Ricco Mortensen

About the author

Ricco Mortensen is an expert in online business and entrepreneurship, speaker and author with a uniquely European flair.

He's worked his way up through the ranks - from McDonald's cashier in Denmark to one of Europe's most esteemed experts in entrepreneurship.

His strengths lie in his endearing personality, with a knack for innovative and logical problem-solving, conjuring up and executing big ideas, and most importantly — sharing his ingenious business solutions with clients, students and friends — while having a heck of a lot of fun in the process.

To be fair, climbing the ladder to success hasn't always been a bed of roses.

Ricco has travelled through hell and high water to get to where he is today, and he celebrates these challenges, because now he can teach people how to avoid making the mistakes he did.

In 1997 Ricco started his very first business — building computers and websites and online shops for clients.

Some of Ricco's early entrepreneurial adventures include coming up with cutting edge solutions for various companies and developing SMS reminders for Danish bookstores, libraries, and beauty salons. He even developed a worldwide document scanning service and even a full service intranet for McDonald's.

In 2012 he began teaching online marketing at VIA University College, Denmark's largest university of applied science.

Since then he's been lecturing and teaching as a visiting professor in universities across Europe and at various events.

Today, Ricco is best known for his ability to help aspiring entrepreneurs build successful online businesses.

Ricco loves to help people create great concepts and one of his greatest talents lies in online strategies plus company and tax optimization, helping clients make the most profit from their hard earned money.

To date, he's educated thousands of students and consulted hundreds of clients.

He even runs business bootcamps in exotic locales all over the World.

He's also created the Ricco Mortensen Foundation, a not-for-profit educational organization aimed at teaching as many people as possible how to have entrepreneurial success.

Ricco is a true inspiration for anyone and everyone who wants to succeed as an entrepreneur.

You can read Ricco's full biography and more about the foundation's activities at www.riccomortensen.com.

Acknowledgements

"For those who run an online business, you will learn how to make it into a money maker. Who wouldn't want one of those?"- Bruno Høiberg.

"Keep your ears pointed in the right direction; a lot of gems and important knowledge is given, it can be difficult to take it all in."- John Bakkestrøm.

"Ricco is in a class of his own. Rarely does one meet such competence. Anything he touches can only turn out well."- Mette Langgaard Laursen.

"Ricco has given me invaluable knowledge and fine tuned what I already knew so that I'm bursting with knowledge and ideas on how to succeed as an entrepreneur! Thank you so much - you know your stuff!"- Lise Kryger.

"Ricco gives you the knowledge you can not get through theoretical books written by American professors who receive money for quantity not quality."- Jimmi Zadstov.

Read more acknowledgements at
www.riccomortensen.com.

Mistake #1:

You earn too little, because you work too much

Let me ask you this: Are you working more hours per week as an entrepreneur than you did when you were employed?

You earn roughly the same as when you were employed - or even worse, is it less?

In other words, you work more now that you've started your own business and actually make less money than you did when you had a typical job.

If so, you're already making the first of the eight most fatal entrepreneurial mistakes.

Which is this: You earn too little because you work too much.

Okay, so you earn too little because you work too much, and the reason for this is: you don't outsource your life. You also don't understand exactly what you need to do with your online business in order to make it a success.

Running an online business is a complex thing

You need a cool website, and you need to know good search engine optimization (SEO). Then there's the setting up of a good payment service provider. I recommend Braintree Payments (www.braintreepayments.com) with no start-up or maintenance fees and low transaction fees.

You also need to put into place and execute your social media strategies, create automated email flows, online ad campaigns, and the list goes on and on.

On top of that, you also need to choose the right company structure, in order to pay as little tax as possible, while also ensuring that the risk of running your business is as low as possible.

All the legal stuff needs to be in order, not too mention the accounting, answering the phone, replying to customer emails, and on and on...

No one is a superman who can do all of these things, so please stop trying to be that superman.

You are wasting your precious time

And even worse, it costs you dearly in the long run.

So you sit there late at night, accounting your records and fooling around with your financial program.

While an accountant will cost you money, it costs you far more money to do it all yourself.

Why?

Because this isn't your core talent, unless you're an accountant, of course.

You really need to do what you do best

For example, all the daily bookkeeping for our foundation and all its operating companies is done by Carla.

She sits somewhere in the Philippines and costs 5 USD per hour. I have never met Carla face to face — thanks to Skype and email.

And no, Carla does not speak Danish — that's my native language. While some documents aren't in English, she manages with near perfection.

She's figured out what the local office supply store and phone company are all about, and if something confuses her, she simply figures it out herself, consults google or yours truly.

Carla also manages some of the foundation's projects, does research, calls and emails customers and vendors, does SEO keyword research and many other great things.

Joel, my graphic designer from somewhere in Portugal, has designed this great book cover, come up with all the necessary marketing materials, online ads for the book, and a lot of other great graphic designs for the foundation's activities.

I've never met or even talked with Joel. Email does the trick.

The English version of this book is brought to you by Aimee's word magic and proofreading skills. She can do things with words and texts that I'll never be able to do myself.

Aimee lives some where in Kansas (like Dorothy in The Wizard of Oz), and nope, I've never met Aimee in person, but audio and video Skype combined with emails work for us.

And these are just some of the great people I work with.

There are many tasks to do when running an online business. In the appendix of this book I have listed some of the tasks we have in the foundation.

Pick the ones that are useful to you and make your outsourcing plan.

Finding the right people to work with

How did I find these great people? The foundation and I use an online platform called Upwork (www.upwork.com) for all freelance jobs.

You simply post a job, find the right candidates, and if they do a good job, you keep them. I've had Carla on board for years now.

The consequence of not outsourcing your life, of doing business the old-fashioned way is this:

You never reach your goals and complete your projects.

You don't get to do what you're best at so every day becomes less than fun and much less productive.

You find yourself sitting there at your designated workspace, fooling around with a lot of things that you shouldn't be doing at all. It's expensive and exhausting, and what's more, you're wasting your precious time by doing too much work.

It takes time and you will fuck up

Finding the right people can take some time. And you will fuck up a few times. Follow your gut feeling.

If you feel that a project with someone is taking too long and the result isn't what you expected, then that person is not the right one for you. Move on and find another one.

They need to fit into how you work, think and communicate, not the other way around. You are the one paying so you are allowed to be in charge here!

Be sure to be very specific when you find your outsourcing partners. Don't accept things that are just good enough. You should have an awesome feeling when receiving their work.

If you're running on a low budget

Trade. Simply trade services or products. You are quite good at something special that others would love to have or use.

I do just that with a few people. Take Christina, for example. She gets my skills and I get her fantastic skills helping me with headlines, copywriting and strategies when my brain gets foggy and I'm out of ideas.

I have saved her a lot of money and helped her with her business and she's done the same for me and the foundation.

Be very clear with one another what the agreement you have together is.

Don't make the mistake of ruining either a good friendship or relationship because you weren't clear about the agreement from the beginning.

Be sure to get everything in writing. You help me with this and I help you with that.

What you can do right now

Have a look at your business. Which tasks are you constantly putting off to the last minute?

You know the ones I'm talking about. They're the ones that require so much extra energy to get done that by the time you finally do, you're left feeling totally drained.

Are there any tasks you really shouldn't be doing?

What you need is a really good overview of all the tasks necessary to run your business. From there, you need to figure out what to do yourself and what you need to outsource.

It's about designing your life, keeping all things running smoothly, and making the profit that suits your financial goals.

It's your life and money that make it possible to live the entrepreneurial life you desire.

Mistake #2:

You are sending your customers directly into the hands of your competitors

Are you aware that you're sending the people who would love to purchase your products directly into the hands of your competitors?

Have you built your website based upon what you think is interesting - not what your potential customers actually care about?

The mistake you're making is this

You don't understand what your potential customers' needs are, how they think, and what they might be searching for in search engines like Google.

Your website is not just a brochure. It's a place for your potential customers to learn more about what they're missing and to take action.

If the price and level of information is right for them, they'll make a purchase or contact you for your services.

People are searching with simple words

People who don't know about your company are searching Google with simple words based upon their needs.

If they need a new washing machine, then they search for that.

If they're in the mood for a nice beach vacation in Thailand, then they type in the search phrase, "vacation in thailand."

Are you aware of what a search engine's most important task is?

It's to show the most exciting, most relevant and most popular content. Google and all the other search engines are working from this premise.

This is why you don't get any visitors

The reason you don't get visitors to your website is because you're not working from this premise.

And...

What you've written is simply not interesting enough according to what your potential customers want to read. Yes, so sorry to speak badly about your content writing skills!

What's more - the search engine optimization you're doing is completely wrong. Even worse, you might not even be doing any SEO at all.

What you can do right now

Look at your website. Are each of your web pages built with the intention of explaining your product in a clear and exciting way while also giving your ideal client exactly what they need?

Do you know how to build your landing pages - the pages where your potential customers actually make their purchase?

Be sure to use a good full service web hosting provider like WPEngine (www.wpengine.com) with WordPress or use a web shop system like Shopify. (www.shopify.com). These services are easy to manage and also make it easy to do your search engine optimisation.

You should familiarize yourself with how to do SEO in order to get more customers easily coming to your website.

I highly recommend using the SEO PowerSuite software from Link-Assistant (www.link-assistant.com) that truly covers all your needs.

It might seem daunting to start, but once you've had your first eye-opening SEO experience, you'll be wondering why you didn't do this long ago.

Mistake #3:

You talk to people who will never be your customer

Are you aware that you might be wasting time talking to the wrong customer?

You may even be talking to the wrong people out of fear of talking to the right ones.

You have no control over your audience and have not even defined your niche and personas.

Your niche is intended to make you stand out from the crowd, and when your niche is clearly defined, you'll know how to communicate with your ideal customers.

Let me give you an example

The niche for the Ricco Mortensen Foundation is this: Entrepreneurs who can and will, but do not know how.

This phrase is defined by who I personally want to help and never get tired of working with. At the same time, this is the target audience for the foundation.

The word "can" in the sentence, means people who can actually afford our services and who are able to learn at the level we've set for the foundation's activities.

The word "will" means that people already understand that online business is the way of the future, that they are ready and willing to work, and want to make their online success a top priority.

The word "know" describes people who are ready to learn something new and eager to get started, they just don't know the exact steps needed for success.

You need to define your personas

A persona is the person you want as your customer. You then define them by their gender, age, residence, income, marital status, family, interests, politics, environmental awareness, where they have travelled, if they commute, ride a bike and all sorts of other personality traits.

Your persona is your secret weapon for getting everything just right – the way you write emails, website content, social media communication, and online ads.

Your persona needs to feel that your whole brand and look is absolutely perfect for them. If they don't, they just move on.

When you sit there surfing the Internet or Facebook

You respond only to the things that really hit the spot based upon your specific needs or feelings in that moment.

You know the annoying feeling when content doesn't teach you something or when you see some kind of online ad that does nothing for you.

This happens because the sender hasn't clearly defined his niche and/or personas. He or she is targeting the wrong person... you! And they are wasting their money.

You don't want to be that guy or gal, do you?

What you can do right now

Look at your current way of communicating. Are you trying to target as many people as possible in one fell swoop? If so, this is a big no-no!

Do you communicate in the old-fashioned one-to-many manner? If so, stop immediately because this mode of communication doesn't work in the online world.

You need to sit down once and for all and define your personas in order to clarify your niche.

It's even more important that you learn how to use social media platforms, email marketing, landing pages and online ads to segment and catch the exact people you want to target. Not everyone out there.

It's all about working in a focused manner. Any other way is a waste of your time and especially your money.

Mistake #4:

Your website is like a leaky bathtub

Mistake number four is that your website is like a leaky bathtub - the money and customers gush right out.

There are two kinds of websites

Those that act as a conversion machine and those that do not.

When I say conversion machine, think of it it like a cash register in a real store.

Customers come into your lovely shop, but you've forgotten to set up a clear and visible counter with a cash register for customers to pay.

The result is that your customers walk right out of your store, and you've not earned a penny.

If you do the same with your website, it's problematic because your visitors won't do what you want them to do.

Get people to do something

The whole point of having a website is to get people to do something - to perform a specific action.

An action does not necessarily always have to be a purchase or money transaction.

It may be to get people to sign up for your newsletter, be contacted, play a video or something else you would like them to do.

An action in online business is called a conversion.

That's why your website needs to convert. Your website should be a conversion machine.

Each of your web pages needs to get people to make a conversion.

You make your customers confused

It's a problem if you show many different options for making a conversion on each of your web pages. These pages are called landing pages.

Too many choices result in your visitors taking no action at all.

It's you who knows best, so it's you who must decide what it is your soon-to-be-customer should do.

Let me give you an example

If you go to Momondo (www.momondo.com), a flight and hotel search engine, notice how simple and easy they've made their front page and its underlying pages.

There is a clear call-to-action - the button you need to click on. They also have really minimized friction.

Friction is all the unnecessary or intrusive things that make people fail to make a conversion.

The website leads you very clearly to the result. The question is then simply whether or not the price is attractive for the hotel or plane you want to book.

Check out Booking.com (www.booking.com), the Swedish IKEA (www.ikea.com) and the Spanish clothing brand Mango (www.mango.com).

See how simple and clear they make everything for you.

Can you see how easy they make it for the customer to make a conversion?

You need to focus on conversions

The reason why you are not getting enough conversions on your website, or other online activities, is because you do not think with this conversion mind-set.

In addition, you need to write online content that provides value while also minimizing friction.

What you can do about it right now

Have a look at your web pages. Is it perfectly clear to the visitor what they'll receive from each web page?

Now check it again and be totally honest! Imagine that it's your grandma Oda who is seeing your web page for the very first time.

What's the conversion on each web page? Is the text on each page of value and does it clearly describe what your product or service provides?

People purchase things that change their lives. They don't buy a gizmo or service simply to buy it. They buy something because it promises to change their lives in some way. What kind of change are you providing?

Have you removed as many friction points as you possibly can so that you'll get the highest number of conversions possible?

Does your website have a professional design theme that's appealing and just right for your personas - not just something you think looks nice?

A good place to purchase really good themes for cheap are at Themeforest (www.themeforest.net). They also offer good customer support and manuals.

Have you made different versions of your landing pages and do you track which version converts the best?

This is what is called conversion optimization. A great tool to test your website is Visual Website Optimizer (www.vwo.com).

Wouldn't you like your website to be a conversion machine?

Mistake #5:

You think you can sell on social media

Listen to me here. You think you can sell on social media in the traditional manner, and even worse, you're actually trying to do it.

You're thinking in terms of sales

In other words, you only think about selling when you communicate on your social media platforms like Facebook and Twitter.

You have completely misunderstood the reason why and how to communicate on your social media business pages.

Why is this a problem? Because social media is not built for sales!

What I'm referring to here is day-to-day communication on your social media profiles, not online ads - which you also need to do.

You're probably surprised

The problem is that you have not made a declaration of intent that clearly and accurately describes what it is your followers get out of following you.

You have not decided who your target audience is on Facebook, for example. You can not target them all together and at the same time.

This is where you must use your personas, as I have told you about previously.

Let me give you an example

It's from a Facebook page I saw that one of my friends had "liked."

The name of the Facebook page is "The Copenhagen raw and rustic tile shop."

Beneath the page name there needs to be a cool declaration of intent that gets you thinking:

Cool, super exciting, that's something I really need to check out or want to follow.

But what it actually shows is the address of the shop - no inspirational message at all that engages the reader.

As a result, I quickly moved on without following their Facebook page.

Busy busy busy

People are busy and are influenced with all sorts of messages all the time.

You have to catch people based on their interests or needs. Otherwise they will simply not react.

Your social media company pages need to establish long lasting relationships.

You meet someone new, chit chat a bit, share some stories, a few secrets, etc. and then form a relationship.

Try to imagine this

You go to a party at your friend's house. During the evening you sit next to a guy you've not met before.

Let's call him John. The first thing John says is, "why hello. I work as a watch maker, will you buy a watch?"

You'll probably try to find someone else to talk to as soon as possible.

But what if John tells you he's passionate about being a watchmaker, and makes you think it's a cool brand and that it fits your style to the tee?

He's also exciting to listen to, interesting, and you even learn something from him.

He might even give you an attractive sales offer that makes you want to purchase one of his watches.

What you can do in your business right now

How do you communicate with your social media company pages?

Are you trying to sell something most of the time, or have you made the right declaration of intent?

Do you communicate as if you were having an ongoing conversation with a good friend?

Is your declaration of intent designed to communicate directly to your personas?

Do you use a social media planning tool for planning ahead and to better understand your social reach?

Check out BufferApp (www.buffer.com) and Hootsuite (www.hootsuite.com) to help you with social media.

If you don't do this right, you'll wind up spending too much time and money on something that gives you no financial benefit in the long run.

Mistake #6:

Your emails are not as good as you think

The sixth of the eight mistakes I see entrepreneurs making all the time is this:

Your emails are not as good as you think. And you do write email campaigns, don't you?

I hate to break this to you, but your emails are probably quite boring.

And because they're so boring, they're not selling anything at all.

When it comes to writing emails that sell

You need to form a relationship with the readers on your email list and create a flow of emails.

A single email itself will in most cases not sell anything if you have not already built upon a relationship.

People who sign up for your newsletter are waiting to hear from you. That's why they signed up.

When you send out an email

You also need to segment your emails. In other words, you don't want to send the same content to everyone on your list.

In fact, you have many different e-mail lists — not just one.

It's essential that you segment your list based upon which of your products or services a person is interested in and what he or she might have already purchased.

You'll likely have more email lists than you do personas.

Each and every email that your readers receive must be relevant based upon where they are in their buying process.

If you just write emails once in a while without a precise plan for what kind of conversion you want them to perform, then you're wasting your time (and theirs).

It's just non-action chit chat.

And let me tell you this

It's absolutely OK if someone thinks you write too much. Maybe they even find you a bit irritating and wind up taking their name off your list.

They won't purchase your product or service anyway.

You have to build an automated email flow, so that everything runs on autopilot and automatically starts when the person signs up for the newsletter, makes a conversion or purchases a product.

The beauty of this is that you only have to build your email campaigns once.

Email segmentation and storytelling

For example, everyone on the foundation mailing lists is segmented by which web pages they've registered from, the products they're interested in, what they have already purchased, and who opened and clicked on links in specific emails.

Writing texts that sell, and especially in emails, requires you to write like a great storyteller - describing the situation your potential buyer is in to a tee.

You need to write clear content, giving them a good sense of what your product's all about and what kind of change it will provide.

If you feel that writing like a storyteller is difficult, then kindly ask a friend to interview you and ask questions about your product.

Record the interview on your mobile phone and then write it all down — word for word. You'll find your words to be much more exciting to read when you do this.

When you get stuck

If you don't want to bother a friend or still think it's difficult and takes too much energy and time — then it's time for you to outsource this task.

Sometimes I'm completely out of ideas when I need to write a new landing page or a new email campaign. I know what I want to say but for some reason I can't get started.

I can spend days if not weeks getting nothing down on paper. I've learned that when this happens, it's time to call on my word wizard Christina.

Often times, within a half hour she'll have a full set of headlines for me to use. They give me inspiration and are just what I need to get started writing the paragraphs full of great content.

I always send my headlines to my word wizard. I will never ever be able to do the word magic that she can do.

She does what she does best — and I do what I do best.

What you can do right now

Look at the latest emails you've sent out. Do you sound like a storyteller when you write?

Are you completely clear as to what you want your reader to click on and what the conversion is?

What kind of change does your product or service create in your customer's life?

Do you use a professional email marketing system like Campaign Monitor (www.campaignmonitor.com) or MailChimp (www.mailchimp.com)? If you want to get super advanced, check out Infusionsoft (www.infusionsoft.com).

Have you enabled an email popup lead generation tool on your website to get more email subscribers? OptinMonster (www.optinmonster.com) is the tool you need for this.

Do you track what your readers do and don't do and then send out one or more follow up emails based upon this?

Mistake #7:

You are wasting your hard earned money on the wrong online ads

When you create your online ads do you communicate to everyone in the traditional one-to-many broadcast manner used in radio, television and traditional physical advertising?

Are you trying to hit "all of them out there" with the same ad?

Have you tried doing online ads and have the feeling that you're wasting your marketing money while seeing very few if any real results?

Can you say yes to this? If so, then you've already answered the question as to whether or not you're making the seventh mistake which is this:

You are wasting your hard earned money on the wrong online ads.

When working with online advertising

You need to think in a different way when working with online marketing.

You must present your product in a way that fits the life and situation of your persona and their needs.

It might seem logical when I say you have to target people based upon this.

You see, with traditional offline marketing, it's simply not possible to target in such a specific manner.

With online advertising, done just right, you can target in a very specific way — based upon the many details that people voluntarily enter into the social media. You can even detect people's behaviours on Facebook.

Some people share everything on social media. Like where they're traveling when they board the airplane, where they get their hair done, and where they go when out with friends.

You also might list whether you are into pop music or rock, if you have just become single, if you just moved, if you are into guys or girls or both, and on and on.

If your day sucks, you might post that you're feeling depressed. Then Wupti, a commercial with anti depressive medicine pops up...

You might be thinking, "I never ever do this." But people all over the globe are doing just this.

As an online advertiser, this gives you a unique opportunity to really segment and customize your online ads for your various audiences or personas.

Let me give you an example

You are to sell a particular washing machine. A little smart one.

Of course you must be in control of your niche, as well as your personas. Let's just say that you have that all set.

Say hello to Simon. He's 23. He just moved into his own space after having lived at home with mom. Simon now lives in an apartment and is single. He is one of our personas.

So you target Simon on Facebook. Here you can target in on the fact that he just moved, he's single, he's a man and he is 23.

You create an ad text that says something like this:

"Oh no! Now your mother's not around to do your laundry. This washing machine is just for you if you've just moved out of the house. As a bonus, we'll give you a guide on how not to fuck up your laundry and mix colours!"

And then of course you have a picture of a young guy standing with a red sock in one hand and a white shirt in the other.

Now you can take it even further

You can create an ad version targeted at the girl who just moved away from home, the man who has just divorced his wife, or the retired couple who has just moved from their house and into a city apartment.

For those who clicked on the ad and visited your landing page but never made a purchase, you turn off the ad.

Instead, you show a more aggressive ad that approaches Simon's challenge with his laundry.

Another problem with your current online ads is that you don't create different ad variations.

In addition, your ads do not generate revenue many times in return and you don't track the conversions on them.

Take control of your online ads

You have to create and customize your online ads targeted at your personas on Google AdWords, Facebook, Twitter, LinkedIn, etc. depending upon where your personas spend time online.

In addition, you need to show special adjusted ads to those who clicked but did not perform your conversion.

This is called retargeting advertising.

Please remember to evaluate which campaigns provide real value-for-money, and turn off the ads that do not.

Isn't it about time to get it right, to create online ads that actually work and earn money for your business?

What you can do about your online ads right now

Look through them carefully. Now, be honest with yourself...

Are your ads targeted to each persona's interests and needs?

Do you run online ads on various online platforms and evaluate where your personas complete the most conversions?

Do you adjust your ads according to where they are in the conversion flow?

Can you measure exactly how much each of your ad variations are costing you, which ones converts the best and which ones do not?

Are you actively using a retargeting marketing tool to target with special ads to visitors who visited your website but didn't complete your conversions?

Use a great tool like AdRoll (www.adroll.com) to target your visitors from nearly everywhere on the net.

Mistake #8:

You have set the wrong goals in your online business

Over the past several chapters your have learned 7 of the 8 mistakes even the most experienced entrepreneurs make.

Here comes the last. Drumroll, please...

You have set the wrong goals for your online business.

The problem is that you have not designed a complete customer flow from start to finish.

This is when you determine when the customer is influenced for the first time, how many times the customer is influenced after an action and when he or she is not, and what makes the conversion finally happen.

It is often a combination of both social media, emails, landing pages and online ads.

You need to specify on what media platforms you plan to communicate to your personas and in what order.

If you do not design your customer flow, you won't earn the great money you can actually earn with your business.

It's silly not to, right?

Of course it's utopia when everyone follows the full flow to a tee.

But if you do not make a plan and if you don't take the necessary online measures needed, then you will not succeed with your conversions, which should be your primary goal.

Conversions, conversions and more conversions

To get as many conversions as possible, you should familiarize yourself with the actions that create the first, the supporting and the final interaction that makes people convert.

You have to get down and dirty with the statistics following all your online initiatives, and learn what works and what does not.

Statistics, yikes

Yes, I know that you might feel an impending sense of dread when I say the word statistics.

Forget the word statistics. It's the conversions you should look for, and also where you earn the most money.

It suddenly becomes much more fun to look at numbers when it comes to which of your actions equal money in the company bank account.

You need to have a look at the statistics on your website using Google Analytics (www.google.com/analytics/). You also need to look at your online ad campaign statistics on Facebook, Google AdWords and anywhere else you run your ads.

Get started by making a check list

Use this book to ask yourself the critical question that's mentioned in each chapter.

Start from the beginning and make a checklist of the things you need to do or the ones you need to do differently.

This checklist is your plan to get your online business back on track.

If you do the things I teach in this book, you've already taken a huge leap in the direction of more money in the company bank account and living the entrepreneurial life you want.

Get free access to the list of must-use online services

I have spent many years testing and evaluating many online services and applications that make it easier to run an online business.

There are many, many options and some are better than others.

As a thank you for purchasing this book - and to help you on your way - I would like to give you access to my secret list of must-use online services.

And it will not cost you a penny. Please read the instructions below.

Most of the solutions are used by my team and myself for foundation projects and are recommended when we give advise to customers choosing solutions for their businesses.

Also, as I have gradually built up a good amount of followers, I have on your behalf negotiated some good discounts on some of these services and tools.

Check them all out to move as quickly as possible in the direction of your business goals and by all means, make use of the discounts!

Visit this web address to get access to the secret list of must-use online services:

www.riccomortensen.com/secret-list/

Get started making the major changes that will make your business succeed!

Just get started...

Appendix:

Tasks for your online business

Running your online business includes many different tasks. It's quite a complex process and you cannot do everything yourself.

Below you'll find some of the many tasks that I recommend you prioritize. Pick and choose the ones that apply to your business.

And be sure to outsource to reach your goals as soon as possible and live the entrepreneurial life you dream of.

Outsourcing

- Sign up on a freelance portal.
- Create job description posts.
- Find candidates and look at previous reviews.
- Evaluate, continue working or find new freelancers.
- Decide if you are going to recruit the freelancers, and if not, find someone else to do this for you.

Website

- Choose a platform (e.g. WordPress).
- Set up the design template.

- Manage hosting/domains, technical issues, backup, etc.
- Write posts and update content.
- Write general texts for "about us," contact info. etc.
- Create landing pages with copywriting including SEO.
- Set up a legal disclaimer, terms of use, privacy and cookie policy.
- Set up a webshop.
- First time and maintenance of products and prices.
- Set up and manage membership pages.
- Perform split tests by making different versions of your webpages to optimize the conversion rate.

Search Engine Optimization

- Find keyword phrases and monitor search engine ranking.
- Audit your website for errors.
- Link and social media building and monitoring.
- Set up sitemap in Webmaster Tools in Google/Bing.

Email marketing

- Create strategy.
- Set up email marketing system.

- Copywriting - including catchy headlines.
- Build up autoresponder flows.
- Create a freebie to get more email signups.
- Set up email signup forms on your website.
- Set up exit opt-in popups to get more subscribers.
- Follow-up on your email campaign statistics.
- Create specific campaigns based on behaviour.

Text & content

- Translate to languages appropriate for your personas.
- Find your copywriting expert.
- Find someone to proofread your texts.

Graphics

- Find a photographer to take great people or product photos.
- Photo editing e.g. of your online ads and landing page photos.
- Create good looking screen presentations.
- Create a design manual for logo, business cards, email signature, etc.

- Printing of business cards, brochures, posters, roll-ups, etc.

Facebook company page

- Setup your page - tune all settings, including graphics.
- Create a strategy.
- Create your declaration of intent.
- Write and schedule posts.
- Follow-up on the statistics.
- Set up targeted online ads, including conversion tracking.
- Evaluate your online ads that convert best.

Twitter account

- Setup and design of account.
- Post tweets.
- Analyse what tweets work best.
- Set up targeted online ads including conversion tracking.
- Follow up on your converting ads.

LinkedIn personal profile & company page

- Set up both your personal profile and company page.

- Build up a great personal profile showing who you are.
- Set up a descriptive company profile.
- Write articles and post news.
- Set up targeted online ads.

YouTube channel

- Set up a company channel.
- Upload your videos with a good description.
- Evaluate your statistics.

Video

- Video recording.
- Video editing.
- Create a few livestreaming events.
- Upload your videos to YouTube, Vimeo, etc.

Social media monitoring & planning

- Pre-schedule your social media posts within one system.
- Evaluate your social media reach and what platforms work best.

Google AdWords

- Set up regular text ads with keywords.
- Target image ads to specific interests and websites.
- Set up shopping ads if you have a webshop.
- Create video ads and promote them on YouTube.

AdRoll

- Set up your retargeting online ads to show across the whole Internet.

Google Analytics

- Set up your goals/conversions.
- Analyse how you get your conversions.
- Evaluate what marketing activities give you the most value for money.

Customer service

- Manage emails, chat and phone with good service 24/7.
- Decide if you should have local country phone numbers.
- Use a good call centre.
- Set up a hat system.

- Set up an email management and tracking system.
- Create a concept manual.

Legal & payments

- Structure your company setup just right with tax optimization.
- Company formation.
- Insurance - both company and a private health insurance.
- Registration of trademarks/patents.
- Find a good and easy online accounting system.
- Find a reliable accountant.
- Set up your payment processor for online payments.
- Create a business PayPal account.
- Get a good debit/credit card.

Made in the USA
Monee, IL
17 October 2021